WHAT I BELIEVE

TO-DAY AND TO-MORROW

*A List of the Contents of
this Series will be found
at the end of this volume*

WHAT I BELIEVE

BY
BERTRAND RUSSELL

Second Impression (Revised)

London
KEGAN PAUL, TRENCH, TRUBNER & CO., LTD.
New York: E. P. DUTTON & CO.
1925

Printed in Great Britain by
M. F. Robinson & Co., Ltd., The Library Press, Lowestoft

PREFACE

In this little book, I have tried to say
what I think of man's place in the
universe, and of his possibilities in the
way of achieving the good life. In
Icarus I expressed my fears ; in the
following pages I have expressed my
hopes. The inconsistency is only
apparent. Except in astronomy, mankind have not achieved the art of
predicting the future ; in human
affairs, we can see that there are forces
making for happiness, and forces
making for misery. We do not know
which will prevail, but to act wisely
we must be aware of both.

January 1st, 1925   B. R.

TABLE OF CONTENTS

WHAT I BELIEVE

CHAPTER I

NATURE AND MAN

Man is a part of Nature, not something contrasted with Nature. His thoughts and his bodily movements follow the same laws that describe the motions of stars and atoms. The physical world is large compared with Man—larger than it was thought to be in Dante's time, but not so large as it seemed a hundred years ago. Both upward and downward, both in the large and in the small, science seems to be reaching limits. It is thought that the universe is of finite extent in space, and that light could travel round it in a few hundred millions of years. It is thought that matter consists of electrons and protons, which are of finite size, and of which there are only a finite number in the world. Probably their changes are not continuous, as used to be thought, but proceed by jerks, which are never smaller than a certain minimum jerk, The laws of these changes can apparently be summed up in a small number of very general principles. which determine the past and the future of the world when any small section of its history is known.

Physical science is thus approaching the stage when it will be complete, and therefore uninteresting. Given the laws governing the motions of electrons and protons, the rest is merely geo- graphy—a collection of particular facts telling their distribution throughout some portion of the world's history. The total number of facts of geography required to determine the world's history is probably finite ; theoretically, they could all be written down in a big book to be kept at Somerset House, with a calculating machine attached, which, by turning a handle, would enable the inquirer to find out the facts at other times than those recorded. It is difficult to imagine anything less interesting, or more different from the passionate delights of incomplete discovery. It is like climbing a high mountain and finding nothing at the top except a restaurant where they sell ginger-beer, surrounded by fog but equipped with wireless. Perhaps in the time of Ahmes the multiplication-table was exciting.

Of this physical world, uninteresting in itself, Man is a part. His body, like other matter, is composed of electrons and protons, which, so far as we know, obey the same laws as those not forming part of animals or plants. There are some who maintain that physiology can never be reduced to physics, but their arguments are not very convincing and it seems prudent to suppose that they are mistaken. What we call our " thoughts " seem to depend upon the organization of tracks in the brain in the same sort of way in which journeys depend upon roads and railways. The energy used in thinking seems to have a chemical origin ; for instance, a deficiency of iodine will turn a clever man into an idiot. Mental phenomena seem to be bound up with material structure. If this be so, we cannot suppose that a solitary electron or proton can " think " ; we might as well expect a solitary individual to play a football match. We also cannot suppose that an individual's thinking survives bodily death, since that destroys the organization of the brain, and dissipates the energy which utilized the brain-tracks.

God and immortality, the central dogmas of the Christian religion, find no support in science. It cannot be said that either doctrine is essential to religion, since neither is found in Buddhism. (With regard to immortality, this statement in an unqualified form might be misleading, but it is correct in the last analysis). But we in the West have come to think of them as the irreducible minimum of theology. No doubt people will continue to entertain these beliefs, because they are pleasant, just as it is pleasant to think ourselves virtuous and our enemies wicked. But for my part I cannot see any ground for either. I do not pretend to be able to prove that there is no God. I equally cannot prove that Satan is a fiction. The Christian God may exist ; so may the Gods of Olympus, or of ancient Egypt, or of Babylon. But no one of these

hypotheses is more probable than any
other : they lie outside the region of
even probable knowledge, and therefore
there is no reason to consider any of
them. I shall not enlarge upon this
question, as I have dealt with it
elsewhere. *

The question of personal immortality stands on a somewhat different
footing. Here evidence either way is
possible. Persons are part of the
everyday world with which science
is concerned, and the conditions which
determine their existence are discover-
able. A drop of water is not immortal ;
it can be resolved into oxygen and
hydogen. If, therefore, a drop of water
were to maintain that it had a quality
of aqueousness which would survive its
dissolution, we should be inclined to
be sceptical. In like manner we know
that the brain is not immortal, and

* See my *Philosophy of Leibniz*, Chapter XV.

that the organized energy of a living body becomes, as it were, demobilized at death, and therefore not available for collective action. All the evidence goes to show that what we regard as our mental life is bound up with brain-structure and organized bodily energy. Therefore it is rational to suppose that mental life ceases when bodily life ceases. The argument is only one of probability, but it is as strong as those upon which most scientific conclusions are based.

There are various grounds upon which this conclusion might be attacked. Psychical research professes to have actual scientific evidence of survival, and undoubtedly its procedure is, in principle, scientifically correct. Evidence of this sort might be so over-whelming that no one with a scientific temper could reject it. The weight to be attached to the evidence, however, must depend upon the antecedent probability of the hypothesis of survival. There are always different ways of accounting for any set of phenomena, and of these we should prefer the one which is antecedentally least improbable. Those who already think it likely that we survive death will be ready to view this theory as the best explanation of psychical phenomena. Those who, on other grounds, regard this theory as unplausible will seek for other explanations. For my part, I consider the evidence so far adduced by psychical research in favour of survival much weaker than the physiological evidence on the other side. But I fully admit that it might at any moment become stronger, and in that case it would be unscientific to disbelieve in survival.

Survival of bodily death is, however, a different matter from immortality :

it may only mean a postponement of psychical death. It is immortality that men desire to believe in. Believers in immortality will object to physiological arguments, such as I have been using, on the ground that soul and body are totally disparate, and that the soul is something quite other than its empirical manifestations through our bodily organs. I believe this to be a metaphysical superstition. Mind and matter alike are for certain purposes convenient terms, but are not ultimate realities. Electrons and protons, like the soul, are logical fictions : each is really a history, a series of events, not a single persistent entity. In the case of the soul, this is obvious from the facts of growth. Whoever considers conception, gestation, and infancy cannot seriously believe that the soul is an indivisible something, perfect and complete throughout this process. It

B

WHAT I BELIEVE

is evident that it grows like the body, and that it derives both from the spermatozoon and from the ovum, so that it cannot be indivisible. This is not materialism : it is merely the recognition that everything interesting is a matter of organization, not of primal substance.

Metaphysicians have advanced innumerable arguments to prove that the soul *must* be immortal. There is one simple test by which all these arguments can be demolished. They all prove equally that the soul must pervade all space. But as we are not so anxious to be fat as to live long, none of the metaphysicians in question have ever noticed this application of their reasonings. This is an instance of the amazing power of desire in blinding even very able men to fallacies which would otherwise be obvious at once. If we were not afraid of death, I do not believe that the idea of immortality would ever have arisen.

Fear is the basis of religious dogma, as of so much else in human life. Fear of human beings, individually or collectively, dominates much of our social life, but it is fear of nature that gives rise to religion. The antithesis of mind and matter is, as we have seen, more or less illusory ; but there is another antithesis which is more important — that, namely, between things that can be affected by our desires and things that cannot be so affected. The line between the two is neither sharp nor immutable—as science advances, more and more things are brought under human control. Nevertheless there remain things definitely on the other side. Among these are all the *large* facts of our world, the sort of facts that are dealt with by astronomy. It is only facts on or near the surface of the earth that we can, to some extent, mould to suit our desires. And even on the surface of the earth our powers are very limited. Above all, we cannot prevent death, although we can often delay it.

Religion is an attempt to overcome this antithesis. If the world is controlled by God, and God can be moved by prayer, we acquire a share in omnipotence. In former days, miracles happened in answer to prayer ; they still do in the Catholic Church, but Protestants have lost this power. However, it is possible to dispense with miracles, since Providence has decreed that the operation of natural laws shall produce the best possible results. Thus belief in God still serves to humanize the world of nature, and to make men feel that physical forces are really their allies. In like manner immortality removes the terror from death. People

who believe that when they die they
will inherit eternal bliss may be expected
to view death without horror, though,
fortunately for medical men, this does
not invariably happen. It does, however, soothe men's fears somewhat,
even when it cannot allay them wholly.

Religion, since it has its source in
terror, has dignified certain kinds of
fear, and made people think them not
disgraceful. In this it has done mankind a great disservice : *all* fear is bad,
and ought to be overcome, not by
fairy tales, but by courage and rational
reflection. I believe that when I die
I shall rot, and nothing of my ego will
survive. I am not young, and I love
life. But I should scorn to shiver with
terror at the thought of annihilation.
Happiness is none the less true happiness because it must come to an end,
nor do thought and love lose their
value because they are not everlasting.

Many a man has borne himself proudly on the scaffold : surely the same pride should teach us to think truly about man's place in the world. Even if the open windows of science at first make us shiver after the cosy indoor warmth of traditional humanizing myths, in the end the fresh air brings vigour, and the great spaces have a splendour of their own.

The philosophy of nature is one thing, the philosophy of value is quite another. Nothing but harm can come of confusing them. What we think good, what we should like, has no bearing whatever upon what is, which is the question for the philosophy of nature. On the other hand, we cannot be forbidden to value this or that on the ground that the non-human world does not value it, nor can we be compelled to admire anything because it is a " law of nature ". Undoubtedly we are part of nature, which has produced our desires, our hopes and fears, in accordance with laws which the physicist is beginning to discover. In this sense we are part of nature ; in the philosophy of nature, we are subordinated to nature, the outcome of natural laws, and their victims in the long run.

The philosophy of nature must not be unduly terrestrial ; for it, the earth is merely one of the smaller planets of one of the smaller stars of the Milky Way. It would be ridiculous to warp the philosophy of nature in order to bring out results that are pleasing to the tiny parasites of this insignificant planet. Vitalism as a philosophy, and evolutionism, show, in this respect, a lack of sense of proportion and logical relevance. They regard the facts of life, which are personally interesting to us, as having a cosmic significance, not a significance confined to the earth's surface. Optimism and pessimism, as cosmic philosophies, show the same naïve humanism : the great world, so far as we know it from the philosophy of nature, is neither good nor bad, and is not concerned to make us either happy or unhappy. All such philosophies spring from self-importance, and are best corrected by a little astronomy.

But in the philosophy of value the situation is reversed. Nature is only a part of what we can imagine ; everything, real or imagined, can be appraised by us, and there is no outside standard to show that our valuation is wrong. We are ourselves the ultimate and irrefutable arbiters of value, and in the world of value Nature is only a part. Thus in this world we are greater than Nature. In the world of values, Nature in itself is neutral, neither good nor bad, deserving of neither admiration nor censure. It is we who create value, and our desires which confer value. In this realm we are kings, and we debase our kingship if we bow down to Nature. It is for us to determine the good life, not for Nature—not even for Nature personified as God.

CHAPTER II

THE GOOD LIFE

There have been at different times and among different people many varying conceptions of the good life. To some extent the differences were amenable to argument ; this was when men differed as to the means to achieve a given end. Some think that prison is a good way of preventing crime : others hold that education would be better. A difference of this sort can be decided by sufficient evidence. But some differences cannot be tested in this way. Tolstoy condemned all war ; others have held the life of a soldier doing battle for the right to be very noble. Here there was probably involved a real difference as to ends. Those who praise the soldier usually consider the punishment of sinners a good thing in itself ; Tolstoy did not think so. On such a matter, no argument is possible. I cannot, therefore, prove that my view of the good life is right ; I can only state my view, and hope that as many as possible will agree. My view is this :

The good life is one inspired by love and guided by knowledge.

Knowledge and love are both indefinitely extensible ; therefore, however good a life may be, a better life can be imagined. Neither love without knowledge, nor knowledge without love can produce a good life. In the Middle Ages, when pestilence appeared in a country, holy men advised the population to assemble in churches and pray for deliverance ; the result was that the infection spread with extraordinary

[28]

rapidity among the crowded masses of supplicants. This was an example of love without knowledge. The late War afforded an example of knowledge without love. In each case, the result was death on a large scale.

Although both love and knowledge are necessary, love is in a sense more fundamental, since it will lead intelligent people to seek knowledge, in order to find out how to benefit those whom they love. But if people are not intelligent, they will be content to believe what they have been told, and may do harm in spite of the most genuine benevolence. Medicine affords, perhaps the best example of what I mean. An able physician is more useful to a patient than the most devoted friend, and progress in medical knowledge does more for the health of the community than ill-informed philanthropy. Nevertheless, an element of benevolence is essential even here, if any but the rich are to profit by scientific discoveries.

Love is a word which covers a variety of feelings ; I have used it purposely, as I wish to include them all. Love as an emotion—which is what I am speaking about, for love " on principle " does not seem to me genuine—moves between two poles : on the one side, pure delight in contemplation ; on the other, pure benevolence. Where inanimate objects are concerned, delight alone enters in : we cannot feel benevolence towards a landscape or a sonata. This type of enjoyment is presumably the source of art. It is stronger, as a rule, in very young children than in adults, who are apt to view objects in a utilitarian spirit. It plays a large part in our feelings towards human beings, some of whom have charm and some the reverse, when considered simply as objects of aesthetic contemplation.

The opposite pole of love is pure benevolence. Men have sacrificed their lives to helping lepers ; in such a case, the love they felt cannot have had any element of aesthetic delight. Parental affection, as a rule, is accompanied by pleasure in the child's appearance, but remains strong when this element is wholly absent. It would seem odd to call a mother's interest in a sick child " benevolence ", because we are in the habit of using this word to describe a pale emotion nine parts humbug. But it is difficult to find any other word to describe the desire for another person's welfare. It is a fact that a desire of this sort may reach any degree of strength in the case of parental feeling. In other cases it is far less intense ; indeed it would seem likely that all altruistic emotion is a sort of overflow of parental feeling, or sometimes a sublimation of it. For want of a better word, I shall call this emotion " benevolence ". But I want to make it clear that I am speaking of an emotion, not a principle, and that I do not include in it any feeling of superiority such as is sometimes associated with the word. The word " sympathy " expresses part of what I mean, but leaves out the element of activity that I wish to include.

Love at its fullest is an indissoluble combination of the two elements, delight and well-wishing. The pleasure of a parent in a beautiful and successful child combines both elements ; so does sex-love at its best. But in sex-love benevolence will only exist where there is secure possession, since otherwise jealousy will destroy it, while perhaps actually increasing the delight in contemplation. Delight without well-wishing may be cruel ; well-wishing without delight easily tends to become cold and a little superior. A person who wishes to be loved wishes to be the object of a love containing both elements, except in cases of extreme weakness, such as infancy and severe illness. In these cases benevolence may be all that is desired. Conversely, in cases of extreme strength admiration is more desired than benevolence : this is the state of mind of potentates and famous beauties. We only desire other people's good wishes in proportion as we feel ourselves in need of help or in danger of harm from them. At least, that would seem to be the biological logic of the situation, but it is not quite true to life. We desire affection in order to escape from the feeling of loneliness, in order to be, as we say, " understood ". This is a matter of sympathy, not merely of benevolence ; the person whose affection is satisfactory to us must not merely wish us well, but must know in what our happiness consists. But this belongs to the other element of the good life, namely knowledge.

In a perfect world, every sentient being would be to every other the object of the fullest love, compounded of delight, benevolence, and understanding inextricably blended. It does not follow that, in this actual world, we ought to attempt to have such feelings towards all the sentient beings whom we encounter. There are many in whom we cannot feel delight, because they are disgusting ; if we were to do violence to our nature by trying to see beauties in them, we should merely blunt our susceptibilities to what we naturally find beautiful. Not to mention human beings, there are fleas and bugs and lice. We should have

[34]

to be as hard pressed as the Ancient Mariner before we could feel delight in contemplating these creatures. Some saints, it is true, have called them " pearls of God ", but what these men delighted in was the opportunity of displaying their own sanctity.

Benevolence is easier to extend widely, but even benevolence has its limits. If a man wished to marry a lady, we should not think the better of him for withdrawing if he found that some one else also wished to marry her : we should regard this as a fair field for competition. Yet his feelings towards a rival cannot be *wholly* benevolent. I think that in all descriptions of the good life here on earth we must assume a certain basis of animal vitality and animal instinct ; without this, life becomes tame and uninteresting. Civilization should be something added to this, not substituted for it ; the ascetic saint and the detached sage fail in this respect to be complete human beings. A small number of them may enrich a community ; but a world composed of them would die of boredom.

These considerations lead to a certain emphasis on the element of delight as an ingredient in the best love. Delight, in this actual world, is unavoidably selective, and prevents us from having the same feelings towards all mankind. When conflicts arise between delight and benevolence, they must, as a rule, be decided by a compromise, not by a complete surrender of either. Instinct has its rights, and if we do violence to it beyond a point it takes vengeance in subtle ways. Therefore in aiming at a good life the limits of human possibility must be borne in mind. Here again, however, we are brought back to the necessity of knowledge.

[36]

THE GOOD LIFE

When I speak of knowledge as an ingredient of the good life, I am not thinking of ethical knowledge, but of scientific knowledge and knowledge of particular facts. I do not think there is, strictly speaking, such a thing as ethical knowledge. If we desire to achieve some end, knowledge may show us the means, and this knowledge may loosely pass as ethical. But I do not believe that we can decide what sort of conduct is right or wrong except by reference to its probable consequences. Given an end to be achieved, it is a question for science to discover how to achieve it. All moral rules must be tested by examining whether they tend to realize ends that we desire. I say ends that we desire, not ends that we *ought* to desire. What we "ought" to desire is merely what someone else wishes us to desire. Usually it is what the authorities wish us to desire—parents, schoolmasters, policemen, and judges. If you say to me " you ought to do so-and-so " , the motive power of your remark lies in my desire for your approval—together, possibly, with rewards or punishments attached to your approval or disapproval. Since all behaviour springs from desire, it is clear that ethical notions can have no importance except as they influence desire. They do this through the desire for approval and the fear of disapproval. These are powerful social forces, and we shall naturally endeavour to win them to our side if we wish to realize any social purpose. When I say that the morality of conduct is to be judged by its probable consequences, I mean that I desire to see approval given to behaviour likely to realize social purposes which we desire, and disapproval to opposite behaviour. At

present this is not done ; there are
certain traditional rules according to
which approval and disapproval are
meted out quite regardless of consequences. But this is a topic with
which we shall deal in the next chapter.

The superfluity of theoretical ethics
is obvious in simple cases. Suppose,
for instance, that your child is ill.
Love makes you wish to cure it, and
science tells you how to do so. There
is not an intermediate stage of ethical
theory, where it is demonstrated that
your child had better be cured. Your
act springs directly from desire for
an end, together with knowledge of
means This is equally true of all
acts, whether good or bad. The ends
differ, and the knowledge is more
adequate in some cases than in others.
But there is no conceivable way of
making people do things they do not
wish to do. What is possible is to

alter their desires by a system of rewards and penalties, among which social approval and disapproval are not the least potent. The question for the legislative moralist is, therefore : How shall this system of rewards and punishments be arranged so as to secure the maximum of what is desired by the legislative authority ? If I say that the legislative authority has bad desires, I mean merely that its desires conflict with those of some section of the community to which I belong. Outside human desires there is no moral standard.

Thus, what distinguishes ethics from science is not any special kind of knowledge, but merely desire. The knowledge required in ethics is exactly like the knowledge elsewhere ; what is peculiar is that certain ends are desired, and that right conduct is what conduces to them. Of course, if the

definition of right conduct is to make
a wide appeal, the ends must be such
as large sections of mankind desire.
If I defined right conduct as that which
increases my own income, readers
would disagree. The whole effective-
ness of any ethical argument lies in
its scientific part, i.e. in the proof that
one kind of conduct, rather than some
other, is a means to an end which is
widely desired. I distinguish, however, between ethical argument and
ethical education. The latter consists
in strengthening certain desires and
weakening others. This is quite a
different process, which will be
separately discussed at a later stage.

We can now explain more exactly
the purport of the definition of the
good life with which this chapter
began. When I said that the good
life consists of love guided by knowledge, the desire which prompted me

was the desire to live such a life as far as possible, and to see others living it ; and the logical content of the statement is that, in a community where men live in this way, more desires will be satisfied than in one where there is less love or less knowledge. I do not mean that such a life is " virtuous " or that its opposite is " sinful ", for these are conceptions which seem to me to have no scientific justification.

CHAPTER III

MORAL RULES

The practical need of morals arises from the conflict of desires, whether of different people or of the same person at different times or even at one time. A man desires to drink, and also to be fit for his work next morning. We think him immoral if he adopts the course which gives him the smaller total satisfaction of desire. We think ill of people who are extravagant or reckless, even if they injure no one but themselves. Bentham supposed that the whole of morality could be derived from " enlightened self-interest ", and that a person who always acted with a view to his own maximum satisfaction in the long run would always act rightly. I cannot accept this view. Tyrants have existed who derived exquisite pleasure from watching the infliction of torture ; I cannot praise such men when prudence led them to spare their victims' lives with a view to further sufferings another day. Nevertheless, other things being equal, prudence is a part of the good life. Even Robinson Crusoe had occasion to practise industry, self-control, and foresight, which must be reckoned as moral qualities, since they increased his total satisfaction without counterbalancing injury to others. This part of morals plays a great part in the training of young children, who have little inclination to think of the future. If it were more practised in later life, the world would quickly become a paradise, since it would be quite sufficient to prevent wars, which are acts of passion, not of reason. Nevertheless, in spite of the importance of prudence, it is not the most interesting part of morals. Nor is it the part that raises intellectual problems, since it does not require an appeal to anything beyond self-interest.

The part of morality that is not included in prudence is, in essence, analogous to law, or the rules of a club. It is a method of enabling men to live together in a community in spite of the possibility that their desires may conflict. But here two very different methods are possible. There is the method of the criminal law, which aims at a merely external harmony by attaching disagreeable consequences to acts which thwart other men's desires in certain ways. This is also the method of social censure : to be thought ill of by one's own society is a form of punishment, to avoid which most people

[45]

avoid being known to transgress the code of their set. But there is another method, more fundamental, and far more satisfactory when it succeeds. This is to alter men's characters and desires in such a way as to minimize occasions of conflict by making the success of one man's desires as far as possible consistent with that of another's. That is why love is better than hate, because it brings harmony instead of conflict into the desires of the persons concerned. Two people between whom there is love succeed or fail together, but when two people hate each other the success of either is the failure of the other.

If we were right in saying that the good life is inspired by love and guided by knowledge, it is clear that the moral code of any community is not ultimate and self-sufficient, but must be examined with a view to seeing

whether it is such as wisdom and
benevolence would have decreed. Moral
codes have not always been faultless.
The Aztecs considered it their painful
duty to eat human flesh for fear the
light of the sun should grow dim.
They erred in their science ; and perhaps they would have perceived the
scientific error if they had had any
love for the sacrificial victims. Some
tribes immure girls in the dark from
the age of ten to the age of seventeen,
for fear the sun's rays should render
them pregnant. But surely our modern
codes of morals contain nothing
analogous to these savage practices ?
Surely we only forbid things which
really are harmful, or at any rate so
abominable that no decent person
could defend them ? I am not so sure.

Current morality is a curious blend
of utilitarianism and superstition, but
the superstitious part has the stronger

hold, as is natural, since superstition is the origin of moral rules. Originally, certain acts were thought displeasing to the gods, and were forbidden by law because the divine wrath was apt to descend upon the community, not merely upon the guilty individuals. Hence arose the conception of sin, as that which is displeasing to God. No reason can be assigned as to why certain acts should be thus displeasing ; it would be very difficult to say, for instance, why it was displeasing that the kid should be seethed in its mother's milk. But it was known by Revelation that this was the case. Sometimes the Divine commands have been curiously interpreted. For example, we are told not to work on Saturdays, and Protestants take this to mean that we are not to play on Sundays. But the same sublime authority is attributed to the new prohibition as to the old.

It is evident that a man with a scientific outlook on life cannot let himself be intimidated by texts of Scripture or by the teaching of the Church. He will not be content to say " such-and-such an act is sinful, and that ends the matter ". He will inquire whether it does any harm, or whether, on the contrary, the belief that it is sinful does harm. And he will find that, especially in what concerns sex, our current morality contains a very great deal of which the origin is purely superstitious. He will find also that this superstition, like that of the Aztecs, involves needless cruelty, and would be swept away if people were actuated by kindly feelings towards their neighbours. But the defenders of traditional morality are seldom people with warm hearts, as may be seen from the love of militarism displayed by Church

D

dignitaries. One is tempted to think that they value morals as affording a legitimate outlet for their desire to inflict pain : the sinner is fair game, and therefore away with tolerance !

Let us follow an ordinary human life from conception to the grave, and note the points where superstitious morals inflict preventable suffering. I begin with conception, because here the influence of superstition is particularly noteworthy. If the parents are not married, the child has a stigma, as clearly undeserved as anything could be. If either of the parents has venereal disease, the child is likely to inherit it. If they already have too many children for the family income, there will be poverty, underfeeding, overcrowding, very likely incest Yet the great majority of moralists agree that the parents had better not know how to prevent this misery by preventing conception. To please these moralists, a life of torture is inflicted upon millions of human beings who ought never to have existed, merely because it is supposed that sexual intercourse is wicked unless accompanied by desire for offspring, but not wicked when this desire is present, even though the offspring is humanly certain to be wretched. To be killed suddenly and then eaten, which was the fate of the Aztecs' victims, is a far less degree of suffering than is inflicted upon a child born in miserable surroundings and tainted with venereal disease. Yet it is the greater suffering which is deliberately inflicted by Bishops and politicians in the name of morality. If they had even the smallest spark of love or pity for children they could not adhere to a moral code involving this fiendish cruelty.

At birth, and in early infancy, the

average child suffers more from
economic causes than from superstition.
When well-to-do women have children,
they have the best doctors, the best
nurses, the best diet, the best rest,
and the best exercise. Working-class
women do not enjoy these advantages,
and frequently their children die for
lack of them. A little is done by the
public authorities in the way of care
of mothers, but very grudgingly. At
a moment when the supply of milk
to nursing mothers is being cut down
to save expense, public authorities
will spend vast sums on paving rich
residential districts where there is
little traffic. They must know that
in taking this decision they are con-
demning a certain number of working-
class children to death for the crime
of poverty. Yet the ruling party are
supported by the immense majority of
ministers of religion, who, with the Pope

at their head, have pledged the vast forces of superstition throughout the world to the support of social injustice.

In all stages of education the influence of superstition is disastrous. A certain percentage of children have the habit of thinking ; one of the aims of education is to cure them of this habit. Inconvenient questions are met with " hush, hush " or with punishment. Collective emotion is used to instil certain kinds of belief, more particularly nationalistic kinds. Capitalists, militarists, and ecclesiastics co-operate in education, because all depend for their power upon the prevalence of emotionalism and the rarity of critical judgment. With the aid of human nature, education succeeds in increasing and intensifying these propensities of the average man.

Another way in which superstition damages education is through its influence on the choice of teachers. For economic reasons, a woman-teacher must not be married ; for moral reasons, she must not have extra-marital sexual relations. And yet everybody who has taken the trouble to study morbid psychology knows that prolonged virginity is, as a rule, extraordinarily harmful to women, so harmful that, in a sane society, it would be severely discouraged in teachers. The restrictions imposed lead more and more to a refusal, on the part of energetic and enterprising women, to enter the teaching profession. This is all due to the lingering influence of superstitious asceticism.

At middle- and upper-class schools the matter is even worse. There are chapel services, and the care of morals is in the hands of clergymen. Clergymen, almost necessarily, fail in two ways as teachers of morals. They

condemn acts which do no harm, and
they condone acts which do great
harm. They all condemn sexual relations between unmarried people who
are fond of each other but not yet sure
that they wish to live together all their
lives. Most of them condemn birth-
control. None of them condemn the
brutality of a husband who causes his
wife to die of too frequent pregnancies.
I knew a fashionable clergyman whose
wife had nine children in nine years.
The doctors told him that if she had
another she would die. Next year she
had another, and died. No one condemned him ; he retained his benefice,
and married again. So long as clergymen continue to condone cruelty and
condemn innocent pleasure, they can
only do harm as guardians of the morals
of the young.

Another bad effect of superstition
on education is the absence of instruction

about the facts of sex. The main physiological facts ought to be taught, quite simply and naturally, before puberty, at a time when they are not exciting. At puberty, the elements of an unsuperstitious sexual morality ought to be taught. Boys and girls should be taught that nothing can justify sexual intercourse unless there is mutual inclination. This is contrary to the teaching of the Church, which holds that, provided the parties are married and the man desires another child, sexual intercourse is justified however great may be the reluctance of the wife. Boys and girls should be taught respect for each other's liberty ; they should be made to feel that nothing gives one human being rights over another, and that jealousy and possessiveness kill love. They should be taught that to bring another human being into the world is a very serious matter, only to be undertaken when the child will have a reasonable prospect of health, good surroundings, and parental care. But they should also be taught methods of birth-control, so as to insure that children shall only come when they are wanted. Finally, they should be taught the dangers of venereal disease, and the methods of prevention and cure. The increase of human happiness to be expected from sex-education on these lines is immeasurable.

It should be recognized that, in the absence of children, sexual relations are a purely private matter, which does not concern either the State or the neighbours. Certain forms of sex which do not lead to children are at present punished by the criminal law : this is purely superstitious, since the matter is one which affects no one except the parties directly concerned. Where there are children, it is a mistake to suppose that it is necessarily to their interest to make divorce very difficult. Habitual drunkenness, cruelty, insanity are grounds upon which divorce is necessary for the children's sake quite as much as for the sake of the wife or husband. The peculiar importance attached, at present, to adultery is quite irrational. It is obvious that many forms of misconduct are more fatal to married happiness than an occasional infidelity. Masculine insistence on a child a year, which is not conventionally misconduct or cruelty, is the most fatal of all.

Moral rules ought not to be such as to make instinctive happiness impossible. Yet that is an effect of strict monogamy, in a community where the numbers of the two sexes are very unequal. Of course, under such circumstances, the moral rules are infringed. But when the rules are such that they can only be obeyed by greatly diminishing the happiness of the community, and when it is better they should be infringed than observed, surely it is time that the rules were changed. If this is not done, many people who are acting in a way not contrary to the public interest are faced with the undeserved alternative of hypocrisy or obloquy. The Church does not mind hypocrisy, which is a flattering tribute to its power ; but elsewhere it has come to be recognized as an evil which we ought not lightly to inflict.

Even more harmful than theological superstition is the superstition of nationalism, of duty to one's own State and to no other. But I do not propose on this occasion to discuss this matter, beyond pointing out that limitation to one's compatriots is contrary to the principle of love which we recognized as constituting the good life. It is also, of course, contrary to enlightened self-interest, since an exclusive nationalism does not pay even the victorious nations.

One other respect in which our society suffers from the theological conception of " sin " is the treatment of criminals. The view that criminals are " wicked " and " deserve " punishment is not one which a rational morality can support. Undoubtedly certain people do things which society wishes to prevent, and does right in preventing as far as possible. We may take murder as the plainest case. Obviously, if a community is to hold together and we are to enjoy its pleasures and advantages, we cannot allow people to kill each other whenever they feel an impulse to do so. But this problem should be treated in a purely scientific spirit. We should ask simply :

[60]

MORAL RULES

What is the best method of preventing murder ? Of two methods which are equally effective in preventing murder, the one involving least harm to the murderer is to be preferred. The harm to the murderer is wholly regrettable, like the pain of a surgical operation. It may be equally necessary, but it is not a subject for rejoicing. The vindictive feeling called " moral indignation " is merely a form of cruelty. Suffering to the criminal can never be justified by the notion of vindictive punishment. If education combined with kindness is equally effective, it is to be preferred ; still more is it to be preferred if it is more effective. Of course the prevention of crime and the punishment of crime are two different questions ; the object of causing pain to the criminal is presum ably deterrent. If prisons were so humanized that a prisoner got a good education for nothing, people might commit crimes in order to qualify for entrance. No doubt prison must be less pleasant than freedom ; but the best way to secure this result is to make freedom more pleasant than it sometimes is at present. I do not wish, however, to embark upon the subject of Penal Reform. I merely wish to suggest that we should treat the criminal as we treat a man suffering from plague. Each is a public danger, each must have his liberty curtailed until he has ceased to be a danger. But the man suffering from plague is an object of sympathy and commiseration, whereas the criminal is an object of execration. This is quite irrational. And it is because of this difference of attitude that our prisons are so much less successful in curing criminal tendencies than our hospitals are in curing disease.

CHAPTER IV

SALVATION : INDIVIDUAL AND SOCIAL

One of the defects of traditional religion is its individualism, and this defect belongs also to the morality associated with it. Traditionally, the religious life was, as it were, a duologue between the soul and God. To obey the will of God was virtue ; and this was possible for the individual quite regardless of the state of the community. Protestant sects developed the idea of " finding salvation ", but it was always present in Christian teaching. This individualism of the separate soul had its value at certain stages of history, but in the modern world we need rather a social than an individual conception of welfare. I want to consider, in this chapter, how this affects our conception of the good life.

Christianity arose in the Roman Empire among populations wholly destitute of political power, whose national States had been destroyed and merged in a vast impersonal aggregate. During the first three centuries of the Christian Era, the individuals who adopted Christianity could not alter the social or political institutions under which they lived, although they were profoundly convinced of their badness. In these circumstances, it was natural that they should adopt the belief that an individual may be perfect in an imperfect world, and that the good life has nothing to do with this world. What I mean may become plain by comparison with Plato's Republic. When Plato wanted to describe the good life, he described a whole community, not an individual ; he did so in order to define justice, which is an essentially social conception. He was accustomed to citizenship of a Republic, and political responsibility was something which he took for granted. With the loss of Greek freedom comes the rise of Stoicism, which is like Christianity, and unlike Plato, in having an individualistic conception of the good life.

We, who belong to great democracies, should find a more appropriate morality in free Athens than in despotic Imperial Rome. In India, where the political circumstances are very similar to those of Judea in the time of Christ, we find Ghandi preaching a very similar morality to Christ's, and being punished for it by the christianized successors of Pontius Pilate. But the more extreme Indian nationalists are not content

E

with individual salvation : they want national salvation. In this they have taken on the outlook of the free democracies of the West. I want to suggest some respects in which this outlook, owing to Christian influences, is not yet sufficiently bold and self-conscious, but is still hampered by the belief in individual salvation.

The good life, as we conceive it, demands a multitude of social conditions, and cannot be realized without them. The good life, we said, is a life inspired by love and guided by knowledge. The knowledge required can only exist where governments or millionaires devote themselves to its discovery and diffusion. For example: the spread of cancer is alarming — what are we to do about it ? At the moment, no one can answer the question for lack of knowledge ; and the knowledge is not likely to emerge except

through endowed research. Again :
knowledge of science, history, literature,
and art ought to be attainable by all
who desire it ; this requires elaborate
arrangements on the part of public
authorities, and is not to be achieved
by means of religious conversion. Then
there is foreign trade, without which
half the inhabitants of Great Britain
would starve ; and if we were starving
very few of us would live the good life.
It is needless to multiply examples.
The important point is that, in all that
differentiates between a good life and
a bad one, the world is a unity, and the
man who pretends to live independently
is a conscious or unconscious parasite.

The idea of individual salvation,
with which the early Christians consoled
themselves for their political subjection,
becomes impossible as soon as we
escape from a very narrow conception
of the good life. In the orthodox

Christian conception, the good life is the virtuous life, and virtue consists in obedience to the will of God, and the will of God is revealed to each individual through the voice of conscience. This whole conception is that of men subject to an alien despotism. The good life involves much besides virtue—intelligence, for instance. And conscience is a most fallacious guide, since it consists of vague reminiscences of precepts heard in early youth, so that it is never wiser than its possessor's nurse or mother. To live a good life in the fullest sense a man must have a good education, friends, love, children (if he desires them), a sufficient income to keep him from want and grave anxiety, good health, and work which is not uninteresting. All these things, in varying degrees, depend upon the community, and are helped or hindered by political events. The good life must

[68]

be lived in a good society, and is not fully possible otherwise.

This is the fundamental defect of the aristocratic ideal. Certain good things, such as art and science and friendship, can flourish very well in an aristocratic society. They existed in Greece on a basis of slavery ; they exist among ourselves on a basis of exploitation. But love, in the form of sympathy or benevolence, cannot exist freely in an aristocratic society. The aristocrat has to persuade himself that the slave or proletarian or coloured man is of inferior clay, and that his sufferings do not matter. At the present moment, polished English gentlemen flog Africans so severely that they die after hours of unspeakable anguish. Even if these gentlemen are well-educated, artistic, and admirable conversationalists, I cannot admit that they are living the good life. Human

[69]

nature imposes some limitation of sympathy, but not such a degree as that. In a democratically-minded society, only a maniac would behave in this way. The limitation of sympathy involved in the aristocratic ideal is its condemnation. Salvation is an aristocratic ideal, because it is individualistic. For this reason, also, the idea of personal salvation, however interpreted and expanded, cannot serve for the definition of the good life.

Another characteristic of salvation is that it results from a catastrophic change, like the conversion of Saint Paul. Shelley's poems afford an illustration of this conception applied to societies ; the moment comes when everybody is converted, the " anarchs " fly, and " the world's great age begins anew ". It may be said that a poet is an unimportant person, whose ideas are of no consequence. But I am persuaded that a large proportion of revolutionary leaders have had ideas extremely like Shelley's. They have thought that misery and cruelty and degradation were due to tyrants or priests or capitalists or Germans, and that if these sources of evil were overthrown there would be a general change of heart and we should all live happy ever after. Holding these beliefs, they have been willing to wage a " war to end war ". Comparatively fortunate were those who suffered defeat or death ; those who had the misfortune to energe victorious were reduced to cynicism and despair by the failure of all their glowing hopes. The ultimate source of these hopes was the Christian doctrine of catastrophic conversion as the road to salvation.

I do not wish to suggest that revolutions are never necessary, but I do wish to suggest that they are not short cuts to the millennium. There is no short cut to the good life, whether individual or social. To build up the good life, we must build up intelligence, self-control, and sympathy. This is a quantitative matter, a matter of gradual improvement, of early training, of educational experiment. Only impatience prompts the belief in the possibility of sudden improvement. The gradual improvement that is possible, and the methods by which it may be achieved, are a matter for future science. But something can be said now. Some part of what can be said I shall try to indicate in a final chapter.

CHAPTER V

SCIENCE AND HAPPINESS

The purpose of the moralist is to improve men's behaviour. This is a laudable ambition, since their behaviour is for the most part deplorable. But I cannot praise the moralist either for the particular improvements he desires, or for the methods he adopts for achieving them. His ostensible method is moral exhortation ; his real method (if he is orthodox) is a system of economic rewards and punishments. The former effects nothing permanent or important ; the influence of revivalists, from Savonarola downwards, has always been very transitory. The latter—the rewards and punishments—

have a very considerable effect. They cause a man, for example, to prefer casual prostitutes to a quasi-permanent mistress, because it is necessary to adopt the method which is most easily concealed. They thus keep up the numbers of a very dangerous profession, and secure the prevalence of venereal disease. These are not the objects desired by the moralist, and he is too unscientific to notice that they are the objects which he actually achieves.

Is there anything better to be substituted for this unscientific mixture of preaching and bribery ? I think there is.

Men's actions are harmful either from ignorance or from bad desires. "Bad" desires, when we are speaking from a social point of view, may be defined as those which tend to thwart the desires of others, or, more exactly, those which thwart more desires than they assist. It is not necessary to dwell upon the harmfulness that springs from ignorance ; here, more knowledge is all that is wanted, so that the road to improvement lies in more research and more education. But the harmfulness that springs from bad desires is a more difficult matter.

In the ordinary man and woman there is a certain amount of active malevolence, both special ill-will directed to particular enemies and general impersonal pleasure in the misfortunes of others. It is customary to cover this over with fine phrases ; about half of conventional morality is a cloak for it. But it must be faced if the moralists' aim of improving our actions is to be achieved. It is shown in a thousand ways, great and small : in the glee with which people repeat and believe scandal, in the unkind treatment of criminals in spite of clear proof that better treatment would have more effect in reforming them, in the unbelievable barbarity with which all white races treat negroes, and in the gusto with which old ladies and clergymen pointed out the duty of military service to young men during the War. Even children may be the objects of wanton cruelty : David Copperfield and Oliver Twist are by no means imaginary. This active malevolence is the worst feature of human nature, and the one which it is most necessary to change if the world is to grow happier. Probably this one cause has more to do with war than all the economic and political causes put together.

Given this problem of preventing malevolence, how shall we deal with it ? First let us try to understand its causes. These are, I think, partly social, partly physiological. The world,

now as much as at any former time, is
based upon life-and-death competition ;
the question at issue in the War was
whether German or Allied children
should die of want and starvation.
(Apart from malevolence on both sides,
there was not the slightest reason why
both should not survive). Most people
have in the background of their minds
a haunting fear of ruin ; this is
especially true of people who have
children. The rich fear that Bolsheviks
will confiscate their investments ; the
poor fear that they will lose their job
or their health. Every one is engaged
in the frantic pursuit of " security ",
and imagines that this is to be achieved
by keeping potential enemies in
subjection. It is in moments of panic
that cruelty becomes most wide-spread
and most atrocious. Reactionaries
everywhere appeal to fear : in England,
to fear of Bolshevism ; in France, to

fear of Germany ; in Germany, to fear of France. And the sole effect of their appeals is to increase the danger against which they wish to be protected.

It must, therefore, be one of the chief concerns of the scientific moralist to combat fear. This can be done in two ways : by increasing security, and by cultivating courage. I am speaking of fear as an irrational passion, not of the rational prevision of possible misfortune. When a theatre catches fire, the rational man foresees disaster just as clearly as the man stricken with panic, but he adopts methods likely to diminish the disaster, whereas the man stricken with panic increases it. Europe since 1914 has been like a panic-stricken audience in a theatre on fire ; what is needed is calm, authoritative directions as to how to escape without trampling each other to pieces in the process. The Victorian age, for all its humbug, was a period of rapid progress, because men were dominated by hope rather than fear. If we are again to have progress, we must again be dominated by hope.

Everything that increases the general security is likely to diminish cruelty This applies to prevention of war, whether through the instrumentality of the League of Nations, or otherwise ; to prevention of destitution ; to better health by improvement in medicine, hygiene, and sanitation ; and to all other methods of lessening the terrors that lurk in the abysses of men's minds and emerge as nightmares when they sleep. But nothing is accomplished by an attempt to make a portion of mankind secure at the expense of another portion—Frenchmen at the expense of Germans, capitalists at the expense of wage-earners, white men at the expense of yellow men, and so on. Such methods only increase terror in the dominant

group, lest just resentment should lead
the oppressed to rebel. Only justice
can give security ; and by " justice "
I mean the recognition of the equal
claims of all human beings.

In addition to social changes designed
to bring security, there is, however,
another and more direct means of
diminishing fear, namely by a regimen
designed to increase courage. Owing
to the importance of courage in battle,
men early discovered means of increasing it by education and diet—eating
human flesh, for example, was supposed
to be useful. But military courage was
to be the prerogative of the ruling
caste : Spartans were to have more
than helots, British officers than Indian
privates, men than women, and so on.
For centuries it was supposed to be the
privilege of the aristocracy. Every
increase of courage in the ruling caste
was used to increase the burdens on the

oppressed, and therefore to increase the grounds for fear in the oppressors, and therefore to leave the causes of cruelty undiminished. Courage must be democratized before it can make men humane.

To a great extent, courage has already been democratized by recent events. The suffragettes showed that they possessed as much courage as the bravest men ; this demonstration was essential in winning them the vote. The common soldier in the War needed as much courage as a Captain or Lieutenant, and much more than a General : this had much to do with his lack of servility after demobilization. The Bolsheviks, who proclaim themselves the champions of the proletariat, are not lacking in courage, whatever else may be said of them ; this is proved by their pre-revolutionary record. In Japan, where formerly the samurai had a monopoly of martial ardour, conscription brought the need of courage throughout the male population. Thus among all the Great Powers much has been done during the past half-century to make courage no longer an aristocratic monopoly : if this were not the case, the danger to democracy would be far greater than it is.

But courage in fighting is by no means the only form, nor perhaps even the most important. There is courage in facing poverty, courage in facing derision, courage in facing the hostility of one's own herd. In these, the bravest soldiers are often lamentably deficient. And above all there is the courage to think calmly and rationally in the face of danger, and to control the impulse of panic fear or panic rage. These are certainly things which education can help to give. And the teaching of every form of courage is rendered

easier by good health, good physique,
adequate nourishment, and free play
for fundamental vital impulses. Perhaps
the physiological sources of courage
could be discovered by comparing the
blood of a cat with that of a rabbit.
In all likelihood there is no limit to
what science could do in the way of
increasing courage, by example, experience of danger, an athletic, life, and
a suitable diet. All these things our
upper-class boys to a great extent
enjoy, but as yet they are in the main
the prerogative of wealth. The courage
so far encouraged in the poorer sections
of the community is courage under
orders, not the kind that involves
initiative and leadership. When the
qualities that now confer leadership
have become universal, there will no
longer be leaders and followers, and
democracy will have been realized
at last.

But fear is not the only source of malevolence ; envy and disappointment also have their share. The envy of cripples and hunchbacks is proverbial as a source of malignity, but other misfortunes than theirs produce similar results. A man or woman who has been thwarted sexually is apt to be full of envy ; this generally takes the form of moral condemnation of the more fortunate. Much of the driving force of revolutionary movements is due to envy of the rich. Jealousy is, of course, a special form of envy : envy of love. The old often envy the young ; when they do, they are apt to treat them cruelly.

There is, so far as I know, no way of dealing with envy except to make the lives of the envious happier and fuller, and to encourage in youth the idea of collective enterprises rather than competition. The worst forms of envy are

in those who have not had a full life in
the way of marriage, or children, or
career. Such misfortunes could in
most cases be avoided by better social
institutions. Still, it must be admitted
that a residuum of envy is likely to
remain. There are many instances in
history of Generals so jealous of each
other that they preferred defeat to
enhancement of the other's reputation.
Two politicians of the same party, or
two artists of the same school, are
almost sure to be jealous of one another.
In such cases, there seems nothing to be
done except to arrange, as far as possible, that each competitor shall be unable
to injure the other, and shall only be
able to win by superior merit. An
artist's jealousy of a rival usually does
little harm, because the only effective
way of indulging it is to paint better
pictures than his rival's, since it is not
open to him to destroy his rival's

pictures. Where envy is unavoidable, it must be used as a stimulus to one's own efforts, not to the thwarting of the efforts of rivals.

The possibilities of science in the way of increasing human happiness are not confined to diminishing those aspects of human nature which make for mutual defeat, and which we therefore call " bad ". There is probably no limit to what science can do in the way of increasing positive excellence. Health has already been greatly improved ; in spite of the lamentations of those who idealize the past, we live longer and have fewer illnesses than any class or nation in the eighteenth century. With a little more application of the knowledge we already possess, we might be much healthier than we are. And future discoveries are likely to accelerate this process enormously.

So far, it has been physical science

SCIENCE AND HAPPINESS

that has had most effect upon our lives,
but in the future physiology and
psychology are likely to be far more
potent. When we have discovered how
character depends upon physiological
conditions, we shall be able, if we
choose, to produce far more of the type
of human beings that we admire.
Intelligence, artistic capacity, benevolence—all these things no doubt could
be increased by science. There seems
scarcely any limit to what *could* be done
in the way of producing a good world,
if only men would use science wisely.
I have expressed elsewhere my fears
that men may not make a wise use of
the power they derive from science.* At
present I am concerned with the good
that men could do if they chose, not
with the question whether they will
choose rather to do harm.

There is a certain attitude about the

* See *Icarus*.

[87]

application of science to human life
with which I have some sympathy,
though I do not, in the last analysis,
agree with it. It is the attitude of
those who dread what is " unnatural ".
Rousseau is, of course, the great pro-
tagonist of this view in Europe. In
Asia, Lao-Tze has set it forth even
more persuasively, and 2400 years
sooner. I think there is a mixture of
truth and falsehood in the admiration
of " nature ", which it is important to
disentangle. To begin with, what is
" natural " ? Roughly speaking, anything to which the speaker was accustomed in childhood. Lao-Tze objects
to roads and carriages and boats, all
of which were probably unknown in
the village where he was born.
Rousseau has got used to these things,
and does not regard them as against
nature. But he would no doubt have
thundered against railways if he had

SCIENCE AND HAPPINESS

lived to see them. Clothes and cooking
are too ancient to be denounced by
most of the apostles of nature, though
they all object to new fashions in either.
Birth-control is thought wicked by
people who tolerate celibacy, because
the former is a new violation of nature
and the latter an ancient one. In all
these ways those who preach " nature "
are inconsistent, and one is tempted to
regard them as mere conservatives.

Nevertheless, there is something to
be said in their favour. Take for
instance vitamines, the discovery of
which has produced a revulsion in
favour of " natural " foods. It seems,
however, that vitamines can be supplied
by cod-liver oil and electric light, which
are certainly not part of the " natural "
diet of a human being. This case
illustrates that, in the absence of
knowledge, unexpected harm may be
done by a new departure from nature ;

[89]

but when the harm has come to be understood it can usually be remedied by some new artificiality. As regards our physical environment and our physical means of gratifying our desires, I do not think the doctrine of " nature " justifies anything beyond a certain experimental caution in the adoption of new expedients. Clothes, for instance, are contrary to nature, and need to be supplemented by another unnatural practice, namely washing, if they are not to bring disease. But the two practices together make a man healthier than the savage who eschews both.

There is much more to be said for " nature " in the realm of human desires. To force upon man, woman, or child a life which thwarts their strongest impulses is both cruel and dangerous ; in thissense, a life according to " nature " is to be commended with certain provisoes. Nothing could be more artificial than an underground electric railway, but no violence is done to a child's nature when it is taken to travel in one ; on the contrary, almost all children find the experience delightful. Artificialities which gratify the desires of ordinary human beings are good, other things being equal. But there is nothing to be said for ways of life which are artificial in the sense of being imposed by authority or economic necessity. Such ways of life are, no doubt, to some extent necessary at present : ocean travel would become very difficult if there were no stokers on steamers. But necessities of this kind are regrettable, and we ought to look for ways of avoiding them. A certain amount of work is not a thing to complain of ; indeed, in nine cases out of ten, it makes a man happier than complete idleness. But the amount and kind of work that most people have to do at present is a grave evil : especially bad is the life-long bondage to routine. Life should not be too closely regulated or too methodical ; our impulses, when not positively destructive or injurious to others, ought if possible to have free play ; there should be room for adventure. Human nature we should respect, because our impulses and desires are the stuff out of which our happiness is to be made. It is no use to give men something abstractly considered " good " ; we must give them something desired or needed if we are to add to their happiness. Science may learn in time to mould our desires so that they shall not conflict with those of other people to the same extent as they do now ; then we shall be able to satisfy a larger proportion of our desires than at present. In that sense, but in that sense only, our desires will then have become " better ".

SCIENCE AND HAPPINESS

A single desire is no better and no worse, considered in isolation, than any other ; but a group of desires is better than another group if all of the first group can be satisfied simultaneously while in the second group some are inconsistent with others. That is why love is better than hatred.

To respect physical nature is foolish ; physical nature should be studied with a view to making it serve human ends as far as possible, but it remains ethically neither good nor bad. And where physical nature and human nature interact, as in the population question, there is no need to fold our hands in passive adoration and accept war, pestilence, and famine as the only possible means of dealing with excessive fertility. The divines say : it is wicked, in this matter, to apply science to the physical side of the problem ; we must (they say) apply morals to the

human side, and practise abstinence.
Apart from the fact that every one,
including the divines, knows that their
advice will not be taken, why should it
be wicked to solve the population
question by adopting physical means for
preventing conception ? No answer is
forthcoming except one based upon
antiquated dogmas. And clearly the
violence to nature advocated by the
divines is at least as great as that
involved in birth-control. The divines
prefer a violence to human nature
which, when successfully practised,
involves unhappiness, envy, a tendency
to persecution, often madness. I prefer
a " violence " to physical nature which
is of the same sort as that involved in
the steam engine or even in the use of
an umbrella. This instance shows
how ambiguous and uncertain is the
application of the principle that we
should follow " nature ".

SCIENCE AND HAPPINESS

Nature, even human nature, will cease more and more to be an absolute datum ; more and more it will become what scientific manipulation has made it. Science can, if it chooses, enable our grandchildren to live the good life, by giving them knowledge, self-control, and characters productive of harmony rather than strife. At present it is teaching our children to kill each other, because many men of science are willing to sacrifice the future of mankind to their own momentary prosperity. But this phase will pass when men have acquired the same domination over their own passions that they already have over the physical forces of the external world. Then at last we shall have won our freedom.

TO-DAY AND TO-MORROW

Other Volumes in preparation

KEGAN PAUL & CO., LTD., LONDON.

7236 4

ω

FOUR